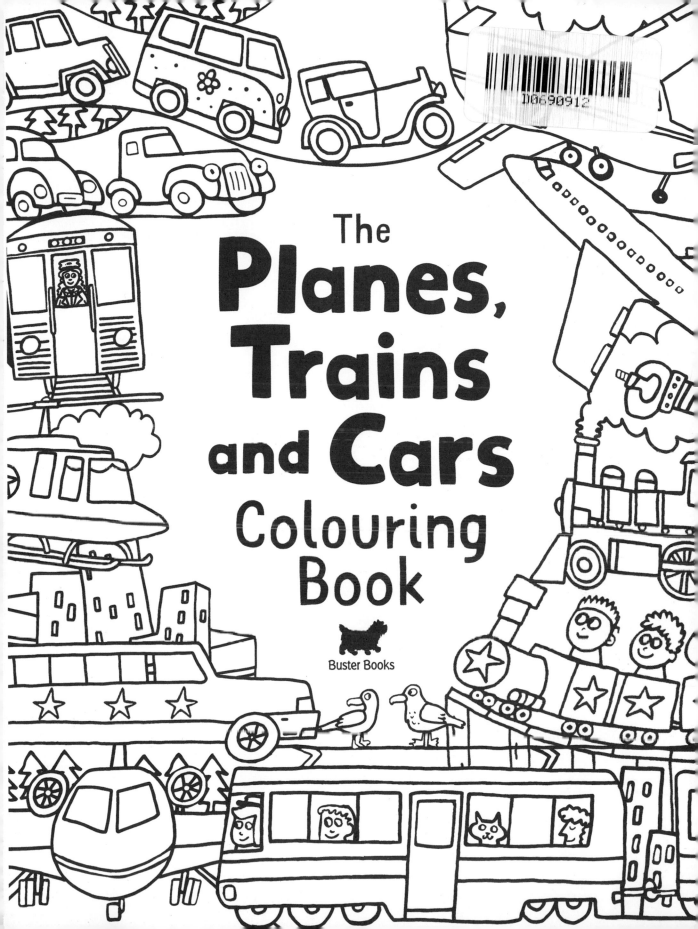

The Planes, Trains and Cars Colouring Book

Buster Books

Illustrated by
Chris Dickason
Cover design by
Angie Allison

Edited by
Sophie Schrey

First published in Great Britain in 2014 by Buster Books,
an imprint of Michael O'Mara Books Limited,
9 Lion Yard, Tremadoc Road, London SW4 7NQ

This updated edition first published in 2021 by Buster Books.

W www.mombooks.com/buster f Buster Books 🐦 @BusterBooks 📷 @buster_books

Copyright © Buster Books 2014 and 2021

A CIP catalogue record for this book is available from the British Library.

ISBN: 978-1-78055-251-4
6 8 10 9 7 5

This book was printed in July 2021 by Leo Paper Products Ltd,
Heshan Astros Printing Limited, Xuantan Temple Industrial Zone,
Gulao Town, Heshan City, Guangdong Province, China.

FSC
www.fsc.org

MIX
Paper from
responsible sources
FSC® C020056

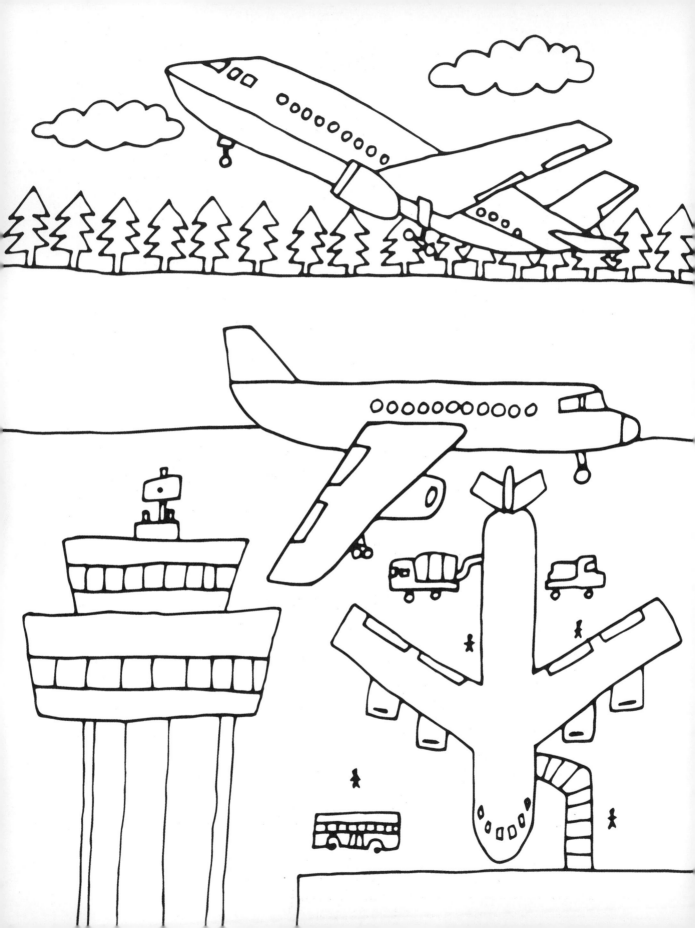

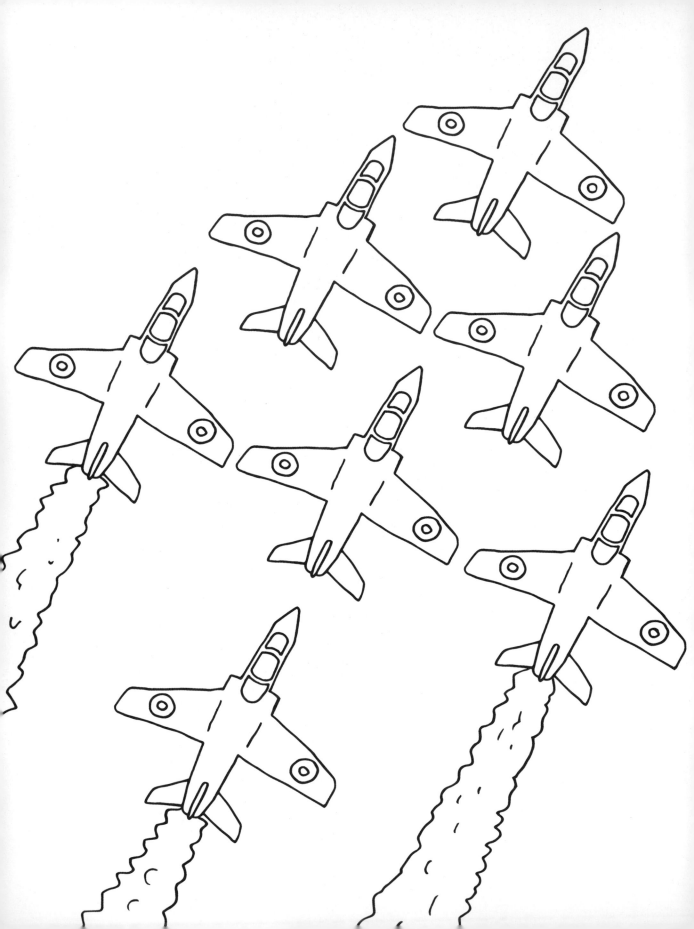

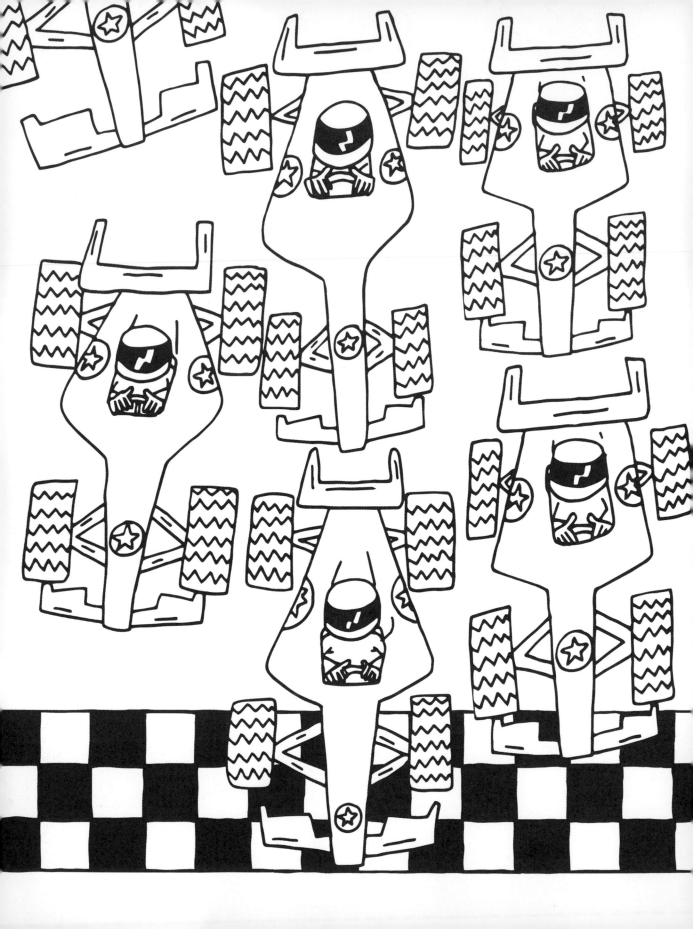

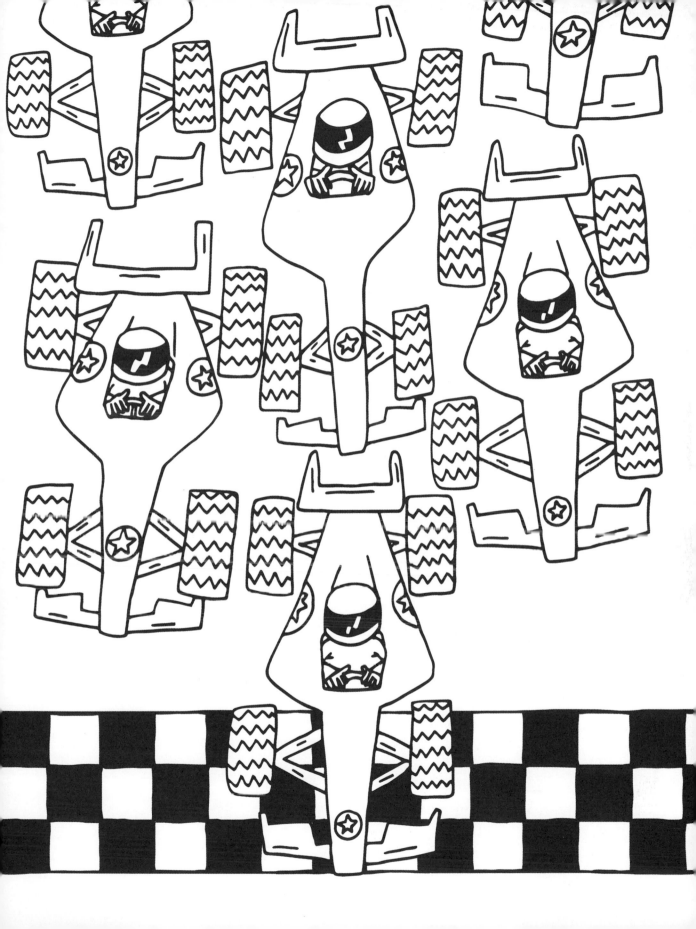

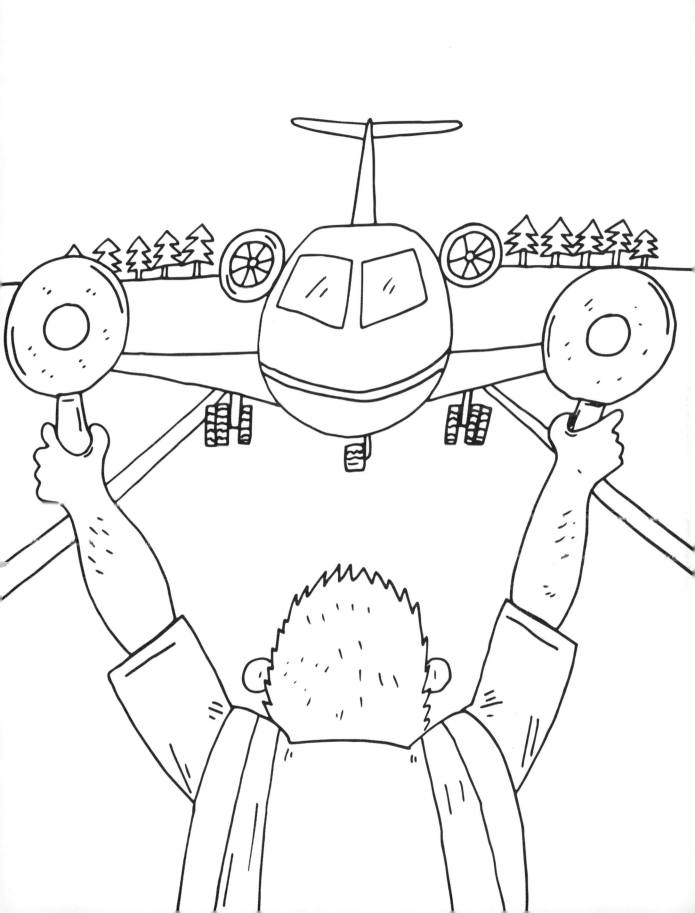